Lia Leads

by Carson Sands
illustrated by Margeaux Lucas

Harcourt
SCHOOL PUBLISHERS

Printed in China

ISBN 10: 0-15-350450-1
ISBN 13: 978-0-15-350450-1

Ordering Options
ISBN 10: 0-15-350333-5 (Grade 3 Below-Level Collection)
ISBN 13: 978-0-15-350333-7 (Grade 3 Below-Level Collection)
ISBN 10: 0-15-357460-7 (package of 5)
ISBN 13: 978-0-15-357460-3 (package of 5)

2 3 4 5 6 7 8 9 10 985 12 11 10 09 08 07

"Lia!" called Mom. "You're going to be late!"

Lia sat in her room. Everything seemed the same, but it wasn't. Sam was gone. Her best friend had moved away.

"Don't worry, Lia," Mom said. "You have other friends."

"I know," Lia murmured.

Sam was her best friend. They had always known each other and done everything together.

Sam was so much fun. She came
up with new games. She made up
stories. She even wrote plays.

Loyal Lia followed along. She
recited the lines Sam made up. She
sang songs that Sam wrote. She
modeled a costume that Sam made.
Now what would she do?

The classroom was filled with voices.

"Hi, Lia," said Alice.

Lia tried to smile. "Hi, Alice."

"Are you signing up for basketball?" asked Alice.

"I don't know," said Lia.

"You should!" said Alice.

Lia wasn't sure. Sam had been a great basketball player. She had led the team. Lia wasn't sure she wanted to play without her.

"All right, class!" said Mr. Harris. "Let's get into our groups."

Lia sat with her group. They were making a map of a town.

"We need a park," said Jen.

"The firehouse needs to be in the center," said Carl.

"What do you think, Lia?" asked Flora.

Sam had always had the good ideas. Lia suddenly felt shy.

"Whatever you want," said Lia.

The rest of the week was the same. She didn't lead a song in music, or choose a book for the class. Sam would have done both.

Lia got a note from Sam.

"Hi, Lia!" wrote Sam. "My new school is fun! I hope you can visit soon."

"I am having fun, too," Lia wrote back. "Basketball won't be the same without you. I hope you can visit soon, too."

The next day, Lia walked slowly into the gym.

"What a coincidence!" said Coach Parker. "I was just thinking about you. You are going to play point guard."

Lia was shocked. That was Sam's position, and the point guard was the leader of the team.

"No, I can't," replied Lia.

"Yes, you can," said Coach Parker in a pleasant voice. "Let's get to work."

Lia tried, but she felt shy calling out plays. She didn't want to direct the other girls.

Soon it was time for their first game. A player on the other team missed a basket. Lia grabbed the ball. She ran down the court. No one was guarding Alice. Lia passed her the ball.

Now the other team had the ball.
Lia told Flora to guard the tall girl near
the basket. Then Lia blocked a shot.
She grabbed the ball and ran for
their basket.

Lia aimed. She shot the ball. It rolled
into the basket. The crowd cheered!

That evening, Lia wrote to Sam.
She told her how she had led the team.
She described the cheers of the crowd.

"That's great!" wrote Sam. "I hope
I'll get to see you play. You're a born
leader, Lia."

Lia smiled. "I guess I am."

Dear Lia,
That's great! I hope
I'll get to see you
play. You're a born
leader, Lia.
Your friend, Sam

Think Critically

1. How does Lia change during this story?

2. How would you describe Sam?

3. Do you think Sam was a good friend to Lia? Why or why not?

4. Why does Coach Parker say it is a coincidence when he sees Lia?

5. What is the setting of the most important scene in this story? Why?

 Social Studies

Make a List In this story, Lia learns about how she can be a leader. What do you think makes a good leader? Make a list of your ideas.

School-Home Connection Lia changed when her best friend moved, and she had to learn to be on her own. What is something that made you change? Share it with a family member.

Word Count: 518